My Grandmother's Backyard Wildlife Sanctuary

By Jane Blythe

To Lily,

Hugs and feathers —

Jane Blythe

the Peppertree Press
Sarasota, Florida

Coming Soon.....
More titles written by Jane

Legend-The Mascot of Parris Island

Simply Splendid Smacks

My Grandmother's Backyard Wildlife Sanctuary — Book 2

For information regarding permission,
call 941-922-2662 or contact us at our website:
www.peppertreepublishing.com or write to:
the Peppertree Press, LLC.
Attention: Publisher
1269 First Street, Suite 7
Sarasota, Florida 34236

ISBN: 978-1-61493-075-4

Library of Congress Number: 2011944516

Printed in the U.S.A.

Printed February 2012

Photos by Jane.

This book is dedicated to my wonderful grandchild,

Alexis,

the sunshine of my life.

Black-crowned
Night Heron

Chapter 1

When I first visited my Grammie's house in Sarasota, Florida last July, it made me sooooo happy!

Not just to see her because she loves me so much and always does fun things with me, and not just for the warm weather and beautiful beaches, but especially because there are SO many birds of Florida's Gulf Coast, right on her lawn! Almost all the time!

When I woke up the first morning, I stepped out on the lanai (luh-neye: what people who live in Florida call their screened-in porches). The back yard was truly beautiful! The little lake looked so pretty and peaceful with green trees and big bushes all around it. There were no loud noises like I hear back home. As a matter of fact, except for the cardinals chirping in a large cluster on one side of the bushes, there wasn't ANY other sound at all. Special!

It begins to get interesting now…as I started to walk out the door, I saw a slightly ridiculous-looking (but very cute) black and white bird sitting on top of the lawn chair. He was on the patio, about eight inches away, just staring into the screen of the lanai. The picture on the left shows just how close he was!

Of course, I called for my grandmother to come and look. I was wondering if she had seen this fellow before. Well, she definitely had, as this **black-crowned night heron** comes to visit her at least two times every day!

Even if she has to go away for a week or so, he (or she) is always there, waiting for her. Grammie said that sometimes he—or is it a she? (we JUST don't know!)—simply is just standing on the lanai near the door waiting for her or sometimes sitting on the birdbath.

One strange fact is that he does not seem to understand that **black-crowned night herons** are mostly **nocturnal** (nok-tur-nl: they stay up all night, but sleep in the daytime). Also they usually are at least a little bit afraid of humans.

This one is so close, we easily can see his bright red eyes peeking from behind his pointy black beak (also called a bill) and he seems to be a little chunky-looking. The top of his head and his back are also black, but his stomach and chest are white and he has yellow legs. Now the really cool part is that he has three narrow, long white feathers called **plumes** (ploomz) that stick out of the back of his head, just above his neck.

Some birds have two feathers, but ours has three. Let me tell you that this is a little funny-looking!! He also makes a loud quarcking sound when he chases other birds away (except for one bird that he cannot chase, and I will tell you about that later).

Although this heron can eat the fish in the lake any time, he prefers to eat canned herring from my grandmother's fingers. It's cool to see and sometimes he even eats it off a special fork we have for him! That is one strange little bird. They are KNOWN for eating mostly at night, so we simply don't know what he is doing here at this time of day. They grow to be about 23 to 26 inches in length, counting the beak, and usually can be found near fresh-water streams or salt marshes. I read that some are even found in Europe.

Chapter 2

We started to walk down to the lake, but a whole bunch of other birds flew in first and looked at us. One was a **great white egret**, about 3½ feet tall.

He ran up towards my grandmother, but hesitated (hez-i-teyt-ed: waited a while) when he saw the **black-crowned heron**, but was all right after a few minutes. He then sat on the birdbath, which was very, very funny to see and it was difficult (hard) for me to stop laughing at him. Let me TELL you— there is no one else in my grandparents' community who has a 3½ foot egret perching on their birdbath!

The **great white egret** has a yellow beak with nice white feathers. He is quite thin, with long black legs and large black feet. He can stand still for a very long time in a lake or on the shore, looking for a fish to eat.

Snowy White Egret

Great White Egret

This bird is supposed to be pretty **common** (lots of this type of bird) in Florida, so you can find them in many places in the state. He always is **solitary** (alone) in our yard though, but is not afraid to be around other types of birds. Sometimes he sticks out his wings and looks angry, which makes some of the other birds run away from him, especially if he makes a funny, hissing sound.

Many egrets grow to be 39 inches or so in height and sometimes when they are flying, their wings measure 50 to 51 inches! That is called their **wingspan**.

What seems very unusual to me is that six or seven different **species** (**spee**-*sheez*: different kinds of birds) will walk TOWARDS my grandmother, but not other people. I believe she has what is called **karma** (**kahr**-m*uh)* with animals and birds. I feel there is some unseen thing in her that attracts them to her. They must know that she truly likes them a lot and is not afraid of them, so they are not afraid of her.

Wood Stork

Chapter 3

Snowy Egret

Next was a very pretty **snowy egret**, which looks quite different from the **great white egret**. It is delicate-looking, only about 1½ feet tall, with yellow feet that look like slippers and beautiful fluffy feathers. The snowy white egret was almost hunted to extinction at one time.

I was going to save the weirdest for last, but I cannot wait—when you see the next pictures, you will think you are looking at something out of the age of the dinosaur. This is an endangered (en-**deyn**-*jerd*: could be wiped out and never seen again) **wood stork**! He is about 40 inches tall and his wings spread out to about five feet when running or chasing every other bird away. His beak is dark-brown and very, very long. The top of his forehead shines and glistens in the sun, as if it were some type of metal. He has a black band that looks exactly like leather, stretching from one eye to the other.

However, his neck is truly more different than anything my grandmother and I have EVER seen on any bird. It is wrinkly, dark-gray and looks just like the armor the knights used to wear into battle many years ago.

The wood stork's legs are very long and his feet have three large pink toes in front, with black toenails that look as if they have just been polished. When he walks towards my grandmother and picks up one foot, his three toes MUSH TOGETHER and look like one loose giant pink blob (see third picture on page 12.) All his muscles must relax or something for this to happen. However, when he puts that foot down, but before he picks up the other one, the three long pink toes are back in place again.

Everyone here is afraid of him and moves away, but he comes towards Grammie and once, she even fed him out of her hand. She said that it didn't hurt, but will not allow me to do it! OH, when he eats the fish she tosses him or the fish in the lake, his beak makes a very loud 'clacking' noise, like two pieces of wood banging together. Usually he will catch his food in mid-air, too.

We tried to measure his beak and it was about as long as his legs!!! He is MY nomination for the strangest-looking bird in my grandmother's backyard wildlife **sanctuary** (**sangk**-*choo*-er-ee: a place of refuge or safety.)

Actually, he is my nomination for the strangest-looking bird I have ever seen *anywhere*!!

Wood Stork

Now, one of the main rules of looking at birds is to watch them from a distance. However, since they always **approach** (come up to) my Grammie, we do not seem to have any choice but to watch them up close, do we?

15

Great
Blue
Heron

Chapter 5

One type of wading bird that comes to Grammie's first thing in the morning is the **great blue heron**, who is very pretty and stately (steyt-lee: with dignity). He waits forever (or so it seems) in one position in the water to find fish to eat.

Sometimes my grandmother feels sorry for him and throws a few crumbs in the lake to attract the fish to that spot. The fish jump all over the **surface** (sur-fis: outer part or top) and then the heron suddenly **thrusts** (stabs) his pointy beak into the water, often coming up with a fish stuck to it! Somehow he is able to turn it around or toss it up in the air and into his mouth, seeming to swallow it in about two seconds! One morning he caught four fish in 25 minutes—that is his record here.

The great heron is about 4 feet tall, and always sits alone here. The bird books also say that he is solitary, calling him the Supreme Power of the wading birds of the Gulf Coast! He is very graceful-looking, with a long reddish-brown neck and even longer reddish-brown legs. His eyes are a very light-yellow, but his beak is gray on top and pink or yellow on the bottom, but VERY pointy—it looks like a little dagger. The top of his head is white and a black band goes around his head from one eye to the other. His body is blue-gray. There is a picture on page 17 of one of his feathers that fell off in our yard.

This is the largest heron in North America (U.S. and Canada) with wings that can spread almost six feet, when he's fully grown.

Oh, I forgot to tell you that Sarasota is on the southwest side of Florida, which is the side that connects with the Gulf of Mexico. It is very hot in the summer and early fall—about in the high 80s to low 90s—and only grows cooler around January and February. Most of our birds stay here year-round.

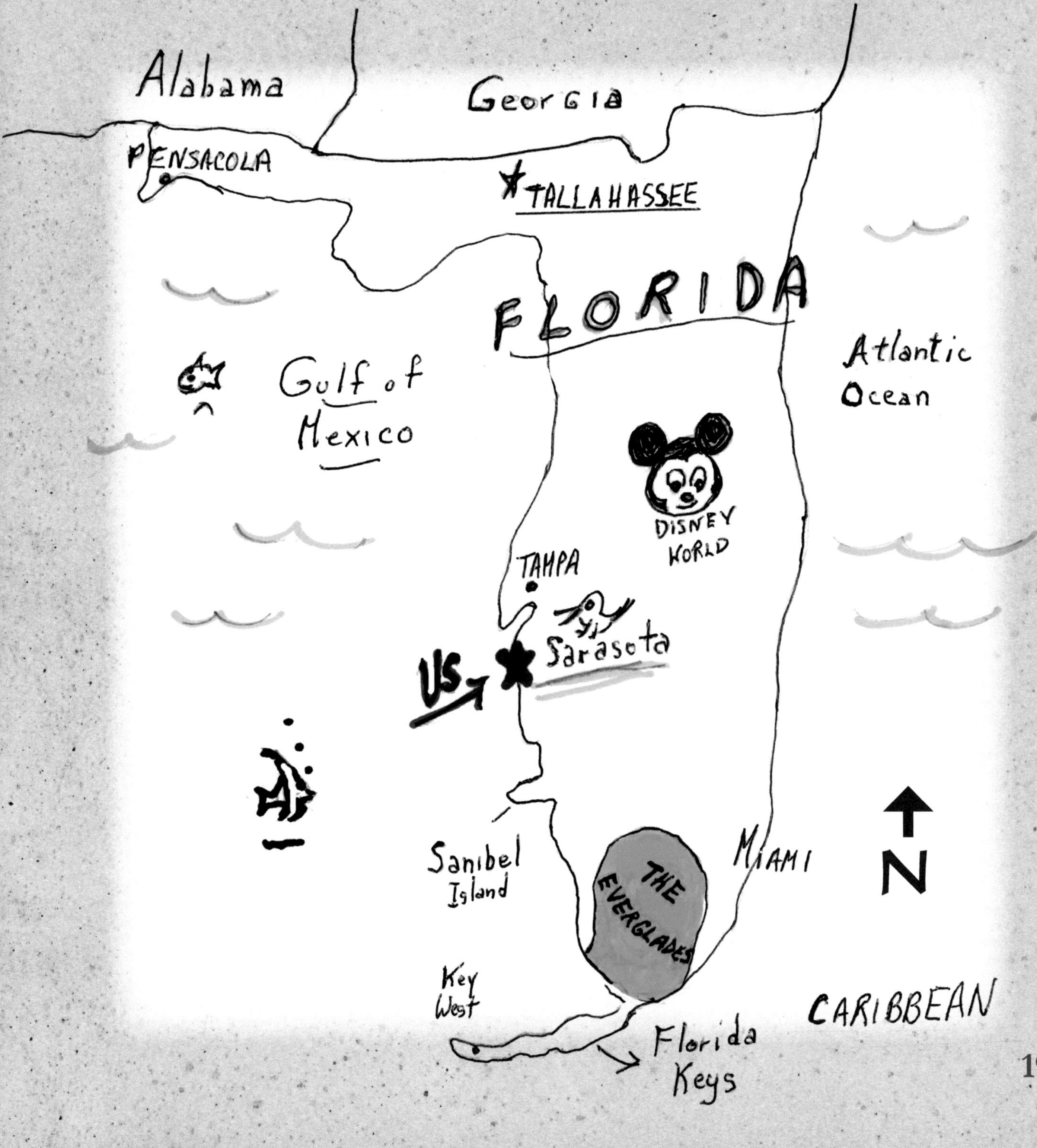

Alabama

Georgia

PENSACOLA

★ TALLAHASSEE

FLORIDA

Atlantic
Ocean

Gulf of
Mexico

DISNEY
WORLD

TAMPA

US →★ Sarasota

Sanibel
Island

THE
EVERGLADES

MIAMI

N

Key
West

CARIBBEAN

Florida
Keys

Chapter 6

One of the cutest birds, in my opinion, is the **ibis** (eye-bis). He has a really orange beak that is long and curves downward with bright orange legs and feet. His feathers are a snow-white color and truly very pretty. They usually are found with a lot of other ibises on the grass or in a pond. We always have at least one of these long-legged wading birds in our yard here.

An ibis will make his first flight when he is about five-weeks-old. When grown, he usually travels in a large flock (group of same animals or birds that travel together). This one, for some reason, is either alone or sometimes with just one or two others, but we have not seen a large group yet. One day we saw an Ibis that was mostly brown.

He is thought to be an immature ibis—kind of like a bird's version of a teenager. (That is my Grandmother's joke— not mine.)

ibis

In another place in Florida where she used to live, my grandmother saw dozens of ibises walking around on the ground, looking for bugs or little things left after a storm. That is really something to see—dozens and dozens of these birds with their long orange beaks, crossing the lawn, looking for food.

I read that the ibis is a very brave bird, as it is thought to be the last bird to fly away before a hurricane comes, but the first bird to return after the hurricane has passed!!

There is one ibis that comes up to Grammie's to visit, often walking around the patio only a few inches from her. He (or she) does not seem to do this with my grandfather or anyone else though—interesting.

The End

(p.s) Don't forget to put fresh water in your bird baths...

Am I a limpkin, a heron or a bittern? What do you think?

Black-crowned Night Heron

Sand Hill Cranes

CPSIA information can be obtained
at www.ICGtesting.com
Printed in the USA
LVIC032114110512

281357LV00002B